BLOODY KANSAS

The Kansas-Nebraska Act of 1854 opened those two territories for settlement. It also said that each territory would decide for itself whether it was to be a slave area or a free area. There was no question of Nebraska becoming a slave state, but both the antislavery forces in the northeastern states and the proslavery forces in the South sent weapons and settlers into Kansas. Each side wanted to win the area for itself, and each harassed and attacked the settlers of the other side. At first the southerners, who were based in neighboring Missouri, had the advantage, but by 1858 the free-staters had won control. Guerrilla warfare continued, however. In January, 1861, Kansas became a free state, but the Civil War, which followed almost immediately, only stepped up the guerrilla warfare. Not until April of 1865 did the Civil War end and guerrilla attacks cease. Peaceable settlers then could enter Kansas safely and before long it was the thriving farm area that had been envisioned when the territory was first opened.

☆   ☆

PRINCIPALS

JOHN BROWN (1800–1859). A ruthless antislavery leader who carried on guerrilla warfare in Kansas and neighboring Missouri until January, 1859. By October of that year he had moved east where he raided Harper's Ferry, Virginia, was captured, and was tried for treason. Found guilty, he was executed on December 2, 1859.

DAVID R. ATCHISON (1807–1886). A proslavery Missouri senator who encouraged Missourians to come and vote illegally in the Kansas elections of 1855. He was a major general of the state militia, and he later led proslavery Missourians in several invasions of Kansas.

JAMES H. LANE (1814–1866). An antislavery leader known as "The Grim Chieftain of Kansas." A militant who led attacks against proslavery settlers, he also raised a Civil War brigade that raided Missouri from Kansas. He was elected one of the first senators from Kansas, and at the height of his career was the most powerful man in the state.

WILLIAM CLARKE QUANTRILL (1837–1865). A guerrilla leader who lived for some time in Kansas, then went to Missouri and became the most famous Confederate raider in the area, leading guerrilla attacks on the Kansas settlements. He was noted for his ruthlessness.

CHARLES ROBINSON (1818–1894). A moderate antislavery leader who was elected the first governor of the state of Kansas and who attempted to restrain the militants. During his term as governor he struggled constantly with Lane and other activists; they dominated his party and he was not nominated for a second term.

A view of Lawrence, Kansas Territory, in the mid-1850's. It was in and around this peaceful town that much of the proslavery and antislavery bloodshed centered for a turbulent decade. (Kansas State Historical Society, Topeka)

A FOCUS BOOK

Bloody Kansas, 1854-65

Guerrilla Warfare Delays Peaceful American Settlement

by James P. Barry

FRANKLIN WATTS, INC.
New York 1972

The authors and publisher of the Focus Books wish to acknowledge the helpful editorial suggestions of Professor Richard B. Morris.

SBN 531-02450-4
Library of Congress Catalog Card Number: 76-152739
Copyright © 1972 by Franklin Watts, Inc.
Printed in the United States of America
1   2   3   4   5

Contents

"For ten years Kansas was a battlefield. From the first year of its settlement late in 1854 to the close of the [Civil] war in 1865, peace was but an empty name as the settlers never knew at what hour they might be attacked. Along the Missouri border the danger was greatest and the deeds of blood perpetrated there were of fearful atrocity."

JUDGE L. D. BAILEY *(who survived that decade)*

BLOODY KANSAS

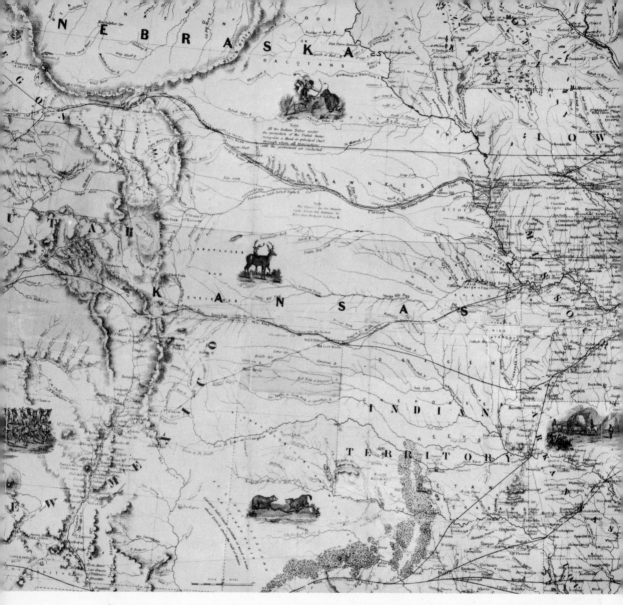

A contemporary map of the Kansas Territory and surrounding areas drawn about 1854. (Kansas State Historical Society, Topeka)

Incident in the Kansas Territory, May, 1856

It was ten o'clock at night when eight men left the camp they had made in a deep grassy ravine at the edge of the timber. They left behind them their wagon and two horses, and walked quietly across the open ground. There was little conversation. The men were dressed in the rough working clothes of the frontier and wore revolvers; each of them also carried a heavy sword.

After walking about a mile they came to a stream called Mosquito Creek. They followed it toward a small cabin that stood in the darkness. At a gesture from the leader of the group, a tall, square-jawed old man, two of them passed by the cabin and went on down the little stream.

As the rest of the men moved toward the house, a dog began to bark fiercely, and as they went closer the snarling animal rushed out at them. One man's sword made a quick chopping motion and the dog was silent. By then the time was nearly eleven o'clock, and two of the men took position as guards, one in front of the dark building and the other behind it. The four remaining men went to the front door and one of them pounded on it.

"Doyle!" he called. There was a muffled answer from inside. The man outside asked where Allen Wilkinson lived. The muffled voice answered again and they could hear Doyle in the cabin moving about and then unlocking the door. As he opened it they thrust their way inside.

Backing James Doyle, the settler, into a corner, the men announced that they were from the "northern army." Mrs. Doyle sat up in bed, confused, and two boys, sixteen and twenty years old, tumbled sleepily out of bed only to be shoved over beside their father and held there at pistol and sword point. The invaders announced that the Doyles were under arrest. A thirteen-year-old girl and a ten-year-old boy huddled frightened in their beds.

First the men took the father out of the house, leaving a guard behind. In a minute they returned for the boys. Mrs. Doyle, weeping, asked them not to take the ten-year-old. After a moment of indecision they went out again, leaving him behind. The last thing the men asked Mrs. Doyle was where the Doyles' horses were, and between sobs she replied that they were grazing on the prairie.

Outside the cabin the men marched the three Doyles some two hundred yards down the road. Using a short, two-edged sword, one of the men suddenly struck the elder Doyle with all his strength. Another cut down one of the sons. The second boy started to run. The man who had killed the father sprinted after the running boy, swung the sword as he came up behind him, and axed him with it. The man then hacked at the fallen body until he was satisfied that the boy was dead.

Meanwhile, the leader of the band, the grim old man, walked over to the body of the father. Perhaps he thought James Doyle was not dead, for the executioner had left quickly to run after the fleeing son. The old man pointed his revolver at the father's corpse and shot it in the forehead.

About a mile farther down Mosquito Creek was the cabin of the Wilkinson family. Mrs. Wilkinson was sick with the measles and was lying awake when she heard a strange noise and woke her husband. Half asleep, he said that it was someone passing on the road. But in a few minutes their dog began to bark as the footsteps approached. Mrs. Wilkinson saw someone pass by the window and then there was a knock at the door.

"Who's that?" she called out.

There was no answer.

She shook her husband awake. He repeated the question, "Who's that?"

A man's voice asked the way to Dutch Henry's — the cabin of another settler.

Wilkinson started to explain.

"Come outside and show us," the voice said.

He started to get up, but his wife would not let him go, so he called out that he could tell them just as well. For a moment the men outside stepped back and there was a whispered conversation among them. Then they returned to the door and asked if Wilkinson was opposed to the northern party.

"I am," Wilkinson told them.

"You're our prisoner. Do you surrender?" said another voice.

"Gentlemen, I do," Wilkinson assured them.

"Open the door."

Allen Wilkinson told them to wait until he made a light. "If you don't open it, we'll open it for you," was the reply. He went over and opened the door. Four men shoved their way into the room and quickly searched the house, asking if there were no other men there; the only others were the Wilkinsons' small children. The men took the one gun and powder flask that were in the house. They told Wilkinson to put on his clothes.

The wife begged them to let him stay with her, saying that she was sick and helpless, and Wilkinson told them that he would stay with her that night and would be there the next day if they wanted him.

The grim old man looked at her and around at the children, and said, "You have neighbors."

She pleaded that she could not leave the house and had no way of getting word to the neighbors.

"It matters not," said the old man, turning away. He told Wilkinson to get ready. Wilkinson started to put on his boots, but the men hurried

[5]

him out without them. One man came back and took two saddles. The woman begged him to let her husband stay with her, but he said that he could not.

Once outside, they moved away with their prisoner. About a hundred and fifty yards from the cabin they stopped, and one of the party struck Wilkinson on the side of the head with a short, heavy sword, and then sliced at his body as he fell. They dragged the corpse to the side of the road.

Mosquito Creek ran into a larger stream called Pottawatomie Creek, and a short distance from that point the road forded the Pottawatomie. The men crossed the ford, were joined by the two others who had gone ahead to scout, and moved to a nearby cabin. About 2:00 A.M. they opened the door, walked in, and went to the bed where James Harris, his wife, and their child lay. Part of the group also went over to the other bed in the one-room cabin, where three men were sleeping; these men were travelers who were staying overnight. Everyone was kept under guard while the invaders ransacked the cabin and took the two rifles and the bowie knife that were there, plus all of the ammunition.

Harris was the first of the settlers that bloody night who recognized the grim, square-jawed commander. He knew him as Old Man Brown. He did not remember that the old man's first name was John, and of course he did not know that the name of John Brown would, before many years, be notorious. But he did know that this man was Brown and he also recognized one of Brown's sons, Owen. (Actually, four of the raiding party were sons of John Brown.)

The men under Brown's command took one of the three travelers out of the house and quizzed him for a time, but then let him return. They cross-examined Harris as to whether he had proslavery leanings, and then spared him. They took a saddle that he had and made him saddle a horse that he was keeping for a neighbor. Then John Brown came back into

[6]

John Brown as he appeared in 1856 during his Kansas raiding days. (Kansas State Historical Society, Topeka)

the house and asked one of the travelers, William Sherman, to go outside with him. Two of Brown's men remained in the house for about fifteen minutes until they heard the small noise made by a pistol cap exploding, then walked out into the darkness.

The next morning Harris and one of the travelers went looking for Sherman, knowing that he had probably been murdered. They found the body about ten o'clock.

I took Mr. William Sherman out of the creek and examined him [Harris later testified]. Mr. Whiteman was with me. Sherman's skull was split open in two places and some of his brains was washed out by the water. A large hole was cut in his breast, and his left hand was cut off except a little piece of skin on one side. We buried him.

[7]

The Beginnings

Civil war came early in Kansas.

The Kansas-Nebraska Act, passed by Congress in 1854, opened those two territories for settlement. It also provided that each of the new territories should decide for itself whether or not it was to have slavery. The uneasy truce between slave and free states was swept aside. Nebraska was sufficiently far north, and at that time sufficiently unattractive to settlers, that the slavery issue did not arise there, but radical elements in both the North and the South concentrated on bringing Kansas into their respective camps. Kansas soon exploded.

The agony that followed had little immediate bearing on slavery. The men who killed each other in Kansas often claimed to be fighting for or against slavery, but most of them were actually fighting for or against southern domination of the territory, which was a somewhat different thing. There were antislavery men on *both* sides, but all those on one side were for northern control of Kansas and all those on the other were for

A typical handbill announcing a meeting on the Kansas-Nebraska Bill (then before Congress) in a small town. (Library of Congress)

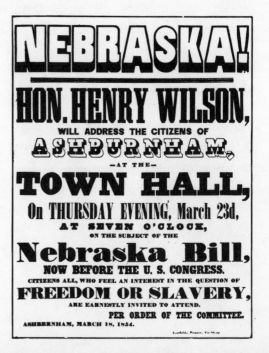

southern control. That was the basic issue. The climate and soil of Kansas were not suited to plantation agriculture, and only a handful of slaves were ever brought into the territory. But if Kansas laws permitted slavery, then Kansas would be dominated by the South and would vote with the southern states. If Kansas laws forbade slavery, then Kansas would be dominated by the North and would vote with the northern states. Thus slavery was a convenient rallying cry, but in fact a North and a South that soon would split apart fought each other in Kansas for the added strength that the extra land and the extra votes of that area would bring, once the territory was settled.

The issue of slavery caused a deep moral reaction in many people of the North and a highly emotional one in many of the South. Men who did not fully understand what was happening in Kansas hurried to join what they thought was the battle over slavery there. Some of the leaders on both sides used the slavery issue, thinking that the public response to it would further their political ends. Then, once the fight began, large numbers of adventurers and a scattering of fanatics and criminals were also attracted to each of the causes. Soon the events in Kansas developed into a guerrilla warfare of move and counter-move, revenge and counter-revenge. But each side defeated itself through its constant use of violence; few real settlers from any part of the country wanted to bring their families into such a battleground or risk their fortunes there; the struggle in Kansas delayed peaceful settlement in that area for a period of ten years.

The territory of Kansas lay immediately west of the state of Missouri, and stretched all the way to Utah. Through it ran the Santa Fe Trail, a major route westward, which began in Missouri and went as far west as what today is Colorado, then turned south to the city of Santa Fe in New Mexico. Missouri, the most populous and vigorous western state, had long been a center of trade; nearly every one of the early western routes used by traders, trappers, or gold hunters ran through that state,

[9]

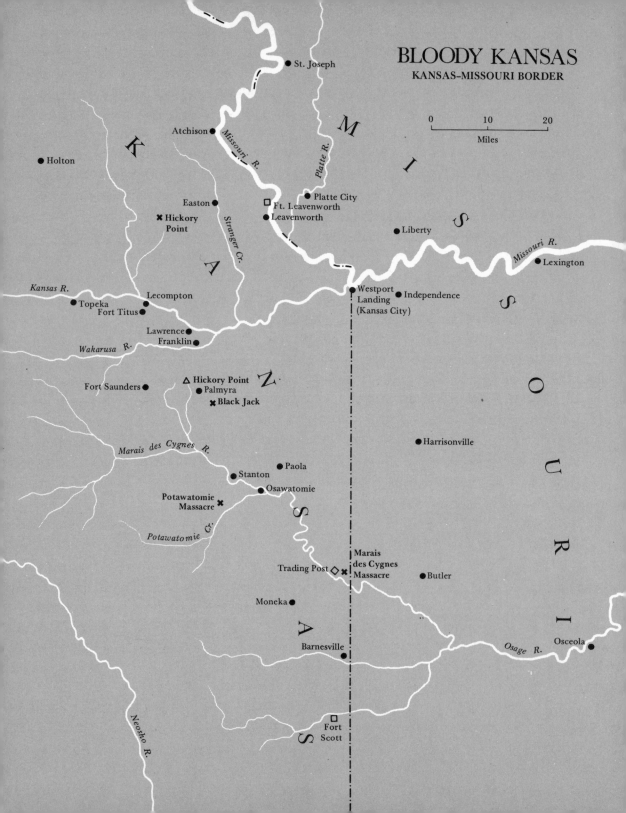

fanning out from its largest city, St. Louis. Towns had sprung up all along the western border of Missouri to outfit the westbound travelers or to send traders among the Indians.

Thus, all roads led east from Kansas to Missouri, and for that reason the newly opened territory was economically dependent on that state. Missouri was also the closest and most logical source of new settlers. It was a slave state. In some ways that was more a frame of mind than a fact; there were few slaves actually owned in the state, and later, in 1861 when the Civil War began officially, that state refused to secede from the Union. Missouri, however, was generally considered to be southern, and was therefore also the logical base from which southern groups could influence events in Kansas.

The abolitionists (people who wanted to abolish slavery) were centered in New England, a long distance away. In order to take a hand in Kansas they organized what they called emigrant aid companies, which provided money to send a number of antislavery men to settle in Kansas and sometimes also provided them with firearms. These abolitionist settlers were strongly against slavery, but most of them had little use for black people and wanted no free Negroes in the territory. They had even less use for the Indians, who were being pushed out of their hunting grounds to let the settlers move in.

In 1855 the first election was held to form a legislature for the territory of Kansas. It was preceded by electioneering of an unusual kind. In Missouri, Senator David R. Atchison, a big, jovial southerner, openly instructed his followers to go into Kansas and vote in the election there. "You can, without exertion, send five hundred of your young men who will vote in favor of your institutions," he told one of his many audiences.

Both sides were prepared for the worst. In a letter to Jefferson Davis, who was then the secretary of war of the United States, Atchison wrote, "We will be compelled to shout, burn & hang, but the thing will soon be

Senator David R. Atchison. (State Historical Society of Missouri)

done." On the other side, Charles Robinson, one of the more moderate northern leaders in Kansas, wrote to a rich New Englander asking for the loan of two hundred rifles and a couple of field pieces "till this question is settled."

There were about fifteen hundred legal voters in Kansas at that time but more than six thousand ballots were cast. The Missourians had followed Atchison's advice and crossed over to vote in large numbers. They elected a prosouthern legislature. The northern party thereupon called a convention at the town of Lawrence, Kansas. This convention repudiated the new legislature on the ground that it had been elected by fraud, and from that time on the northerners referred to it as the "bogus legislature." (The fraud had obviously taken place; what was less obvious was that at this early time there would probably have been more southern than northern votes even if Senator Atchison had told his followers to stay in Missouri.)

During the northern convention James H. Lane, one of the leaders of the northern party, tried hard to get the convention to consider issues that were more applicable to Kansas than was the question of slavery, but the New England abolitionists were the strongest force in the northern ranks, and the convention decided to make slavery the one point in question.

Territorial Governor Andrew H. Reeder called the prosouthern legislature to meet at Pawnee on July 2, 1855. Instead, the legislature defied him, gathered at Shawnee Mission, and passed strong proslavery laws: offices could only be held by proslavery men, any person who asserted that slavery was not legal in Kansas was to be imprisoned at hard labor for not less than two years, and anyone who encouraged or helped a slave to run away was punishable by death. Reeder vetoed the laws; the legislature passed them over his veto. By midsummer the southern group had had enough of Governor Reeder and managed to have him removed on charges of land speculation. (In four years Kansas was to have six governors.)

Handbill announcing a free-state convention at Big Springs on September 5, 1855. (Kansas State Historical Society, Topeka)

In October, the northerners met at Topeka in another convention at which James H. Lane was the presiding officer, and there they drew up a constitution that forbade slavery in Kansas and made it a free state. The following January they elected their own legislature. Kansas then found itself with a proslavery legislature sitting at Shawnee Mission and an anti-slavery legislature sitting at Topeka.

The Murder of Charles Dow

In the meantime, all of these angry and often illegal acts were building up to violence. In November of 1855 the first explosion came.

In the little village of Hickory Point, on the Santa Fe Trail in the eastern part of Kansas, both free-state men and Missourians had taken up claims. At that time there had been no government land survey in the area of Hickory Point. The borders of the Shawnee Indian Reserve, some distance away, had been surveyed, however, and some of the Hickory Point settlers thought that if the Shawnee survey were used as a base, a line could be run from it to their district. Their claims could then be based on this survey and they felt that it would be very close to the official government survey that would come later. Other settlers preferred to wait until the official survey came in.

Charles W. Dow, a settler who had come from Ohio, had a claim next to that of Franklin M. Coleman, who had originally come from Virginia but had lived in both Iowa and Missouri. They had agreed upon the location of the boundary between their two claims. But then a group of the settlers, Dow among them, decided to survey their claims on the basis of the Shawnee line. This survey caused the boundary of Dow's property to move two hundred and fifty yards west — onto land that Coleman believed was his. Coleman continued to cut timber on the land, Dow objected, and they had a violent argument.

On November 21 Dow was returning from a trip to the blacksmith shop at Hickory Point. He was walking, carrying the wagon part he had taken to be repaired, when he met Coleman, who was at the home of one of the settlers along the way. Coleman had his shotgun. As Dow passed, Coleman hailed him and the two of them walked down the road together, talking. As they went, they resumed their argument over cutting the timber. They walked as far as Coleman's house, where he stopped while Dow continued along the road. Coleman raised his gun to his shoulder and pulled the trigger; the gun misfired. Dow, hearing a slight noise but not realizing what it was, turned around and said something to Coleman. Coleman again raised his gun and this time it fired.

Dow fell over backward, hit by nine lead slugs. Two of them cut his jugular vein, the others went into his chest. Several went completely through his body. Coleman immediately went to Shawnee Mission and placed himself in the custody of the sheriff, Samuel J. Jones. The body lay in the road until nearly dark when a friend of Dow's named Jacob Branson came to find him.

At this point, what had been a personal argument between two settlers became the murder of a northerner by a southerner. A number of free-state men armed themselves and set out to find Coleman. Some thirty of them searched the Coleman house, despite the protests of Mrs. Coleman. They then moved on to the houses of the neighbors and from one of them learned that Coleman had gone to Shawnee Mission. Not only was the place some distance away, but it had also become a headquarters of the southern faction. The free-staters could not pursue Coleman there.

The murder took place on the twenty-first. By the twenty-sixth the free-staters had whipped up indignation to the point where a hundred people, a number of them from Lawrence, which was the base of the northern party, gathered at the place where Dow had fallen. They listened to violent speeches; Dow's friend, Jacob Branson, was one of the leaders. The meeting then passed several resolutions, among them the appointment of a "vigilance committee" to bring Coleman "as well as those connected with him" to justice. Of course no one else had been connected with him in his private argument, but there were other southerners in the community who were connected with his political views. After the meeting, several members of the vigilance committee burst into Coleman's house and set fire to it, but others restrained them and put out the fire.

One of the southern settlers who lived at Hickory Point was H. H. Buckley. On the twenty-sixth he was visiting Shawnee Mission. He and Branson had had frequent political arguments. Perhaps he really was afraid of Branson and the vigilantes who were roaming the town; perhaps he merely saw a good chance to injure Branson. In any event, he swore out a warrant charging that Branson had threatened his life. Sheriff Jones and a number of other armed men thereupon escorted Buckley back to Hickory Point, arriving shortly after seven that evening.

They went to Branson's home, broke down the door, and poured into the house. Jones put his cocked pistol to Branson's chest and announced that he was under arrest. The group permitted him to dress, then took him out and mounted him on a mule. After several stops for friendly drinks at the houses of other southerners, Jones and his men started out after dark to take Branson to the settlement of Lecompton, a southern town that was the nearest place where there was a magistrate.

When Sheriff Jones went to arrest Branson, he and his people made no secret of what they were about, so that by the time they were taking him out of town a group of northerners had assembled some distance outside Hickory Point, waiting for them. As Jones and his posse moved down the road, the northerners lined up across it, armed with whatever

Sheriff Samuel J. Jones of Shawnee Mission. (Kansas State Historical Society, Topeka)

they had been able to find. Two of them had squirrel rifles, some had pistols, and at least one had only a handful of heavy stones. As the sheriff's party rode up and saw the waiting men, they halted. One of them asked, "What's up?"

"That's what we want to know," answered one of the northerners, firing his pistol in the air. Another of the group called out to ask if Branson was there. Branson answered that he was.

"Come out of that," one of the free-staters told him.

Branson demurred; he said that they would shoot him if he did.

"Let them shoot and be damned," said an angry northerner. "We can shoot too."

There was a general cocking of guns on both sides. Then Branson kicked his mule in the ribs and rode over to the other group. Nobody shot. The two groups stood there arguing for nearly an hour and finally Sheriff Jones took his men and went off, leaving Branson behind.

That night the houses of Coleman and Buckley were burned to the ground.

[17]

The Wakarusa "War"

The men who had rescued Branson decided to take him in honor to Lawrence, the free-state center. One of them owned a drum, a sword, and some additional military equipment. He kept the drum for himself and passed out the rest of the items to the others. They headed north to Lawrence, arrived there about daybreak, and proceeded into town with the drummer leading the way, beating a rousing tattoo. The citizens of the place, as it turned out, were not at all enthusiastic about the idea of taking a prisoner away from a law officer, and one of the northern leaders, Charles Robinson, told them that they should not have come there. But after marching around the streets for a while they stopped to hold a meeting, gathering as many people as they could.

In the course of the meeting, Branson was called upon to speak. With tears running down his cheeks he related the story of what had happened to him, saying that his wife was now alone in their house and he had no idea what was happening to her. He also offered to leave the town of Lawrence immediately, as he did not want the residents to suffer because of him. Then the group of rescuers asked the meeting for a resolution endorsing their action. Instead, the meeting rejected that idea unanimously. Finally, ten men were appointed to consider the matter and to report at another meeting later that afternoon. The final result was a lukewarm statement that the citizens pledged themselves to "the resistance of lawlessness and outrage at all times."

Meanwhile, Sheriff Jones went to the town of Franklin, from which most of his posse had come. It was a prosouthern area and the story of the Branson rescue was told and retold there with growing indignation. Jones sat down and wrote one message to southern leaders in Missouri and another to Governor Shannon of Kansas Territory, saying that Branson had

[18]

been released by a party of forty armed desperadoes. He added, "You may consider an open rebellion as having already commenced, and I call upon you for *three thousand* men to carry out the laws."

The governor panicked. Without any further investigation he sent out orders calling the state militia to active duty, saying "Reliable information has reached me that an armed military force is now in Lawrence, or in that vicinity, in open rebellion against the laws of this Territory." He also called upon Colonel E. V. Sumner, who commanded the regular army troops of the First United States Cavalry at Fort Leavenworth. Sumner told him that he could do nothing until he received orders from Washington, and the governor immediately telegraphed the President, asking for Sumner's regiment.

Numbers of Missourians poured into Kansas and joined the Kansas militia. Even whole militia units came from Missouri and put themselves under Sheriff Jones's orders. These men were armed with weapons issued

Old engraving entitled "Missourians Going to Vote" shows a band of tough "border ruffians" on their way to cast proslavery ballots in Kansas. (Photo by Cushing)

them either from arsenals in Missouri before they left that state, or from government supplies in Kansas after they arrived there. Many of the weapons remained in the private hands of the southerners throughout the following months. Many of the men were good citizens responding to what they thought was the call of duty. Others were men of the sort that had gained the name of "Border Ruffians" — hard characters who were waiting for a chance to be legalized bandits and who did not mind robbing a few Kansas settlers while they waited. Most of them gathered in a camp on the Wakarusa River, east of Lawrence, anxiously waiting to attack the town. Another group was concentrated in the southern stronghold of Lecompton, northeast of Lawrence.

By this time Governor Shannon was having second thoughts. He wrote to Sheriff Jones that he expected the President to issue orders placing the regular army troops under his control and therefore "you will wait until I obtain the desired orders before attempting to execute your writs," adding that the force that Jones had gathered "had better remain at a distance, until it can be ascertained whether their aid will or will not be needed." The governor pointed out to Jones that the men at Lawrence would be more apt to respect the authority of the federal soldiers. He did not add what he probably was also beginning to see, that the First Cavalry would be under considerably better control than the undisciplined body that was gathering at the Wakarusa.

Sheriff Jones replied that his volunteers were beginning to get restless and that he would like to get on with the job. But in the meantime, two citizens of Lawrence managed to reach Governor Shannon with their side of the story. Shannon then completely reversed his attitude; he sent off word to Colonel Sumner that he needed his cavalrymen at Lawrence as soon as possible to protect that town against the men gathered at the Wakarusa. Sumner again answered that he was ready to move as soon as he received orders from Washington.

A sketch of James H. Lane. (Kansas State Historical Society, Topeka)

In Lawrence the citizens began to prepare for an attack by quickly throwing up fortifications. The northern leader James H. Lane, a tall, lean man who had raised a regiment of volunteers in Indiana for the Mexican War and had served during that war as a colonel, took charge of the defenses. Rifles sent from New England were issued to those who had none. Most of these weapons were Sharps rifles, the new breech-loaders invented by Christian Sharps and manufactured in New England. They could be fired much more rapidly than the muzzle-loaders used by the southerners and gave their owners a considerable advantage. The men of Lawrence drilled and practiced military formations. Nearby free-state men came into town to help with the defense. On December 7 Governor Shannon visited Lawrence; the people there met him courteously and he conferred with their leaders. He insisted that they must obey the laws of the legislature, which they termed "bogus laws," and that they must give up their weapons. The first demand the northern leaders considered impossible and the second one, under the circumstances, unreasonable. Shannon, disappointed, went back to Camp Wakarusa.

[21]

Free-staters manning their battery about 1855. (Kansas State Historical Society, Topeka)

The men there were in growing bad humor, but some of their leaders agreed with the governor that they should try to reach a settlement with the northern leaders from Lawrence. The two groups met at Franklin, and after a long discussion drew up a treaty in which both sides agreed to resolve their differences according to law. Thereupon Governor Shannon issued orders disbanding both the men at Wakarusa and the "Enrolled Citizens of Lawrence," as well as directing Sheriff Jones to send home his posse. What came to be known as the Wakarusa "War" had ended.

But meanwhile, on December 7, a one-horse wagon rolled into Lawrence carrying the equipment of the five men who trudged beside it. Their leader wore two revolvers in his belt and carried a rifle. A Lawrence paper carried the story:

> About noon, Mr. John Brown, an aged gentleman from Essex County, N.Y., who has been a resident of the Territory for several months, arrived with four of his sons — leaving several others at home sick — bringing a quantity of arms with him, which were placed in his hands by Eastern friends for the defense of the cause of freedom. . . . A company was organized and the command given to Mr. Brown for the zeal he had exhibited in the cause of freedom both before and since his arrival in the Territory.

A Restless Winter

After the armistice, John Brown and his sons went home as did the other volunteers who had come to defend Lawrence. But Brown had made his first appearance on the scene, armed and ready to fight, and would come again.

The Missourians also went home, speeded on their way by the start of one of the bitterest winters men could remember. On December 8, the area near Lecompton in which the southerners were camped in one night experienced rain, hail, snow, and winds ranging up to tornado strength. Most of the men did not have tents. This stormy beginning was followed by deep snows and temperatures as low as thirty degrees below zero. It was no winter for guerrilla operations.

Even so, there were some disturbances. In January, 1856, the free-staters held their own election for state officers and members of the legislature. In several places southern groups, a number of them imported from Missouri, attempted to stop what they considered illegal voting. The offices of a pronorthern newspaper in the town of Leavenworth were destroyed by a mob. Ballot boxes were seized in a number of places and there were several fights.

In the town of Easton, during these election disturbances, two opposing groups fired at each other. A southerner was killed and two northerners were wounded. Later, the southern band captured a few of the northerners, in time freeing all but the captain of the northern group. When some of the cooler heads suggested taking him to Leavenworth for trial they were shouted down by the mob, which broke down the door of the room in which he was confined, dragged him out into the open, and attacked him with hatchets and knives. He died soon afterward.

In spite of the disturbances, the free-staters formed a legislature and elected state officials, including a "governor," Charles Robinson. As the governors of territories were appointed by the President of the United States, this step was a direct challenge to federal authority.

A portrait of Charles Robinson, first governor of Kansas. (Kansas State Historical Society, Topeka)

The Shooting of Sheriff Jones

With the approach of spring, more northern settlers came into the territory, bringing with them rifles. Other rifles were shipped in to the free-staters. The congregation of the Reverend Henry Ward Beecher, a noted eastern abolitionist, subscribed money to give each member of one settlement a Bible and a rifle. Beecher himself was quoted as saying that in Kansas there was more moral power in a rifle than in a Bible. The rumor spread that rifles were being shipped into the territory in boxes marked "Bibles." Thereafter rifles sent from the northeastern states were known to both sides as "Beecher's Bibles."

Senator Atchison of Missouri turned to the slave states for help, and in April a force of three hundred men, organized as a military unit, left Alabama for Kansas. They brought no women or children. Georgia, South Carolina, and Tennessee also sent contingents of settlers. The two sides were speeding toward a collision.

Sheriff Jones visited Lawrence several times that winter. On April 19 he saw one of the men who had rescued Branson, and Jones arrested him. A crowd immediately surrounded the officer and his prisoner, but the townspeople acted as though the whole thing was a joke. They stole the sheriff's pistol and jostled him, allowing his prisoner to escape. The sheriff left town in a bad mood and returned the next day with a posse of four men. He saw another of the Branson rescuers and pounced on him; the man promptly hit him. Jones retired again without a prisoner, muttering angry threats.

The sheriff reported these events to Governor Shannon, who asked Colonel Sumner at Fort Leavenworth to send an officer and several men of the United States Army with Jones to help him make the arrests. Sumner had by this time received instructions from Washington to help

[25]

Shannon, and so he sent a Lieutenant McIntosh and ten soldiers. At that time he also wrote a letter to the mayor of Lawrence, saying that he would not take sides in the controversy, but that the laws of the government must be obeyed.

With his escort of cavalry, Jones arrived in Lawrence on the twenty-third of April. He arrested six men and had them locked up and guarded by the troopers. The sheriff and Lieutenant McIntosh shared a tent that night. In the early evening, as Jones moved around outside the tent, someone shot at him but missed. Later in the evening a man stumbled into the tent, apparently drunk, and took a seat. When he was ordered to leave he did so. Evidently he was not actually drunk, but was noting where the sheriff sat, for shortly after he left, two shots were fired through the canvas; one struck Jones, injuring his spine, and he fell, paralyzed.

It appeared that he was mortally wounded. He was quickly moved to a hotel and a doctor was called. (In time he recovered, but for the rest of his life he was slightly paralyzed.) The responsible citizens of Lawrence, horrified, gathered in a meeting the next morning, denounced the act, and offered five hundred dollars as a reward for the arrest of the gunman.

Colonel Sumner and a detachment of the First Cavalry soon arrived outside Lawrence and made camp there. After an investigation Sumner decided that for the time being things were under control in Lawrence, but before returning to Fort Leavenworth he wrote a letter to Charles Robinson, the free-state governor, saying, "The recent attempt made upon the life of Sheriff Jones will produce great excitement throughout the Territory and on the Missouri frontier, and I consider it of the utmost importance that every effort should be made by your people to ferret out and bring to justice the cowardly assassin. It is not too much to say that the peace of the country may depend on it, for, if he is not arrested, the

[26]

act will be charged by the opposite party upon your whole community." Robinson answered that every effort was being made to find the would-be assassin. The guilty man never was identified, however.

The Beating of Charles Sumner

On the national scene, meanwhile, the North and the South were reacting to dispatches from their partisans in Kansas. On May 19 and 20 of 1856 Senator Charles Sumner of Massachusetts, a stern man with a deep moral commitment to the destruction of slavery, made a lengthy speech in Washington before packed senate galleries, a speech to which he later gave the title, "The Crime Against Kansas." It was an account as he saw it of the developments unfolding in the new territory, and it was presented with the righteous certainty of the crusader. The speech gave no hint of the complex events that were really taking place there; as far as Sumner was concerned, the North was fighting against slavery in that distant frontier area and everything the northerners did had to be right.

A portrait of Senator Charles Sumner of Massachusetts, an ardent abolitionist. (Photo by Cushing)

Most of what Charles Sumner said was quite dull, as self-righteous political speeches are apt to be. Then, however, he began a personal attack on one of the southern leaders, Andrew Butler of South Carolina, who happened to be absent. "The Senator from South Carolina has read many books of chivalry, and believes himself a chivalrous knight, with sentiments of honor and courage. Of course he has chosen a mistress to whom he has made his vows, and who, although ugly to others, is always lovely to him; although polluted in the sight of the world, is chaste in his sight — I mean the harlot Slavery."

Many Washingtonians were startled by the personal attack on Butler; most southerners there were outraged. One southerner living in the nation's capital was a member of the House, Preston Brooks, who was also a relative of Andrew Butler's. Brooks decided that it was his task to punish Sumner. At this time challenges issued by southern legislators to their northern colleagues were fairly common, but most northerners simply refused to duel; and anyway, Brooks reflected, Sumner was certainly no gentleman. A challenge was used only between social equals. The proper thing to do, in the code of the southern cavalier, was to administer a beating to Sumner.

Congressman Brooks went to the Senate when it was not in session and found Charles Sumner there at work at his desk. A lady was visiting the chamber and the fiery Brooks waited until she left; he observed such social amenities with care. Then he strode to Sumner's desk, said that he had come to punish him for his slander, and struck him with a walking stick. He continued to strike repeatedly while the older man, in pain and confusion, stood up so violently that he pulled his desk from the floor to which it was bolted. The attacker broke his cane and continued in a frenzy to hit his stunned victim with the butt of it until two other members of the House ran in and pulled him away. A number of senators, most of them from the South, watched the exhibition but did not interfere.

Contemporary cartoon shows Congressman Preston Brooks caning Senator Sumner on the Senate floor. (Photo by Cushing)

What the two halves of the country had been doing with such frequency in Kansas had now taken place in the Senate Chamber as well. An uninformed and foolishly insulting verbal attack on the one side had been answered by an inexcusable physical attack on the other. As a sign of the unhappy condition to which the nation had come, however, almost no one saw the event in that light. Throughout the North, Sumner was hailed as a pure hero; throughout the South, Brooks was cheered as the chivalrous ideal. Both men were subsequently re-elected by their constituencies, but it was three years before the martyred Sumner was enough recovered to return to his duties regularly.

[29]

The Sacking of Lawrence

Early in May, a United States grand jury met at the southern strong-hold of Lecompton. It indicted for treason many of the prominent free-state leaders because of their activities in setting up the separate northern legislature and electing state officers. The judge of the United States District Court gave the United States marshal Israel B. Donalson warrants to arrest these men. Donalson sent a deputy marshal to Lawrence to carry out the arrests. By the time the deputy arrived, most of the men he was looking for had disappeared, but he did find one of them, who warned him that he and his friends would strongly resist any move to make an arrest. The deputy marshal decided not to risk the attempt.

The two key leaders of the northern party were outside Kansas Territory at this time. James H. Lane was traveling through the North gathering money, settlers, and weapons. Charles Robinson had just left Kansas on a similar errand, but he was arrested in Missouri and was returned to Kansas by the Missouri authorities.

Meanwhile, on May 11, Marshal Donalson issued a proclamation "To the People of Kansas Territory," saying that attempts to make arrests in Lawrence had been resisted "by a large number of the people of Lawrence," and calling for the law-abiding citizens of the territory to gather at Lecompton as soon as possible "in numbers sufficient for the execution of the law" in order to proceed to Lawrence to arrest the men indicted by the grand jury. Missourians had already begun to assemble along the Kansas border. On May 13, 1856, the people of Lawrence sent a letter to Governor Shannon pointing out that "large numbers" of the citizens had *not* resisted the deputy marshal and offering to provide the marshal with a posse to help him make the arrests directed by the court. Shannon did not respond.

[30]

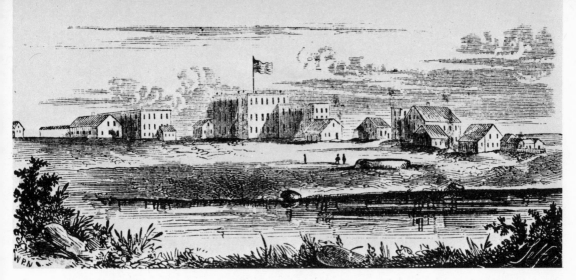

A sketch of Lawrence made about a week before the town was sacked in May, 1856, by proslavery forces. Note breastworks in foreground near riverbank for defense purposes. (Photo by Cushing)

The southern forces continued to gather. The various armed contingents that had come from southern states joined the marshal's posse, as did militia units from Missouri, who brought with them two cannon. Former Senator Atchison of Missouri came to ride with the posse. (Atchison's bid for re-election in Missouri had been defeated.) Inevitable fights took place between the border-ruffian element in the southern force and some of the free-state people. Two young northerners were killed and the bloody corpse of one of them was carried to Lawrence, where excitement ran high.

On May 20 the posse of eight hundred men arrived outside Lawrence. The citizens there had decided to follow the law meticulously and to make no resistance. All of the women and children had been sent out of town to take shelter in a nearby ravine. Late in the morning a deputy United States marshal rode into town with ten assistants and gathered a small posse of citizens, who obeyed him and helped him arrest three men. The posse was then dissolved and Donalson and Atchison were invited to

[31]

dine at the Free State Hotel, a building that was owned by one of the emigrant aid companies and was the headquarters of the northern party.

On May 21 Sheriff Jones, who had recovered sufficiently from his wounds to be able to ride, left the posse's camp accompanied by twenty of his men and rode into Lawrence. He pulled up in front of the Free State Hotel and called for a representative of the citizens to come out. One man, S. C. Pomeroy, stepped out, greeted the sheriff in a friendly manner, and shook his hand. Jones then demanded that the citizens give up all of their weapons, and allowed five minutes for them to agree. Pomeroy answered that the arms of the citizens were their private property and each of them would have to make his own personal decision, but that he would surrender the cannon that belonged to the town. He led Jones and his men to the place where the cannon was stored and turned it over to them.

Ruins of the Free State Hotel in Lawrence after the raid in May. (Photo by Cushing)

By three o'clock all eight hundred men had moved into Lawrence. Some of them destroyed the presses and offices of the two newspapers. Others emplaced cannon across the street from the Free State Hotel while one man, to the accompaniment of cheers, climbed to the roof and fastened a South Carolina flag there. Then the cannon opened fire, putting about fifty shots into the building. When the shots failed to knock it down the men swarmed inside, piled the furniture together, and set fire to it. Finally the walls collapsed, to a tremendous cheer from the crowd.

The posse quickly degenerated into a mob, and there is no evidence that any of its leaders tried to control it. It broke into homes and stores, carrying away whatever it liked. After plundering the house of Charles Robinson, the mob set fire to it. Finally the men rode away. After it was all over, the correspondent of the *Missouri Republican* wrote happily to his proslavery newspaper, " The day, Wednesday, the 21st of May, was truly a May day; the sun scarcely ever shone more brilliantly and all, save Lawrence, looked fresh with life and glory. But that ill-fated town appeared deserted, doomed."

The Pottawatomie Massacre

When the people of Lawrence began to realize that a southern attack was coming, some of them again sent out calls for help to abolitionist groups elsewhere. Among those that responded were the Pottawatomie Rifles, an irregular band consisting of settlers from an area some thirty miles south of Lawrence. The commander of this group was John Brown, Jr. Among its members were John Brown, Sr., and several of his other sons. As they moved toward Lawrence they were met by two messengers, the first of whom told of the destruction of that town and the second of whom brought orders to go no farther because federal troops were now in control of the place and food was scarce. On May 23, 24, and 25 the men under John Brown, Jr., camped near the place where they received these messages.

After the messenger arrived with the news that Lawrence had been sacked, the elder John Brown called for volunteers who would obey his orders. His son, John Brown, Jr., the commander of the force, objected. The elder Brown persisted. John Brown, Jr., pointed out that it would weaken the force if his father took part of it away, and he warned against doing anything rash. The older man continued to call for volunteers and seven responded. Four were his sons and one was his son-in-law. Members of the unit warned the old man to be careful. Without heeding them he led his volunteers away.

Old John Brown and his party returned to Mosquito Creek, which was in the Pottawatomie area not far from the place where he lived with one of his sons. After some minor changes in plans, the elder Brown and his followers proceeded with the murders of the Doyles, Wilkinson, and Sherman. These acts came to be lumped together under the name of "The Pottawatomie Massacre."

Many reasons for the killings have been suggested. The character of John Brown was a strange one. He had engaged in over twenty businesses in six different states and had failed in nearly all of them; he had been involved in many court cases over the past years because he had not paid debts, because he had not paid the wages of men who had worked for him, and because he had had other dishonest dealings. Also, there had been insanity in his family. It is difficult to understand why such a man acted as he did, but some reconstruction of his motives may be possible.

The elder Brown was merely a soldier in the force commanded by one of his sons. The men who organized this irregular company must have felt when they put the son in command that he was a more responsible

[34]

A portrait of John Brown in later years. After his famous raid on Harper's Ferry in 1859 he was tried, convicted, and hanged that same year. (Photo by Cushing)

person than the father; the older man could not have been happy about their feeling. After all, he had been appointed captain of a militia company on that first trip to Lawrence, and he was a man who liked to be dramatic. The news that his son's unit was too late to help Lawrence evidently suggested to old John Brown a chance to take control for himself. But his call for volunteers only produced seven, five of whom were from his own family.

All of the victims of John Brown and his raiding party had been members of a grand jury, or officials or employees of the court, when the

United States District Court sat in the Pottawatomie area on April 21 and 22. The Pottawatomie Rifles had stacked arms outside the courtroom and gone in in a body, and one of them had presented a written question to the judge asking if he intended to enforce the laws of "the Territorial Legislature, so-called." Judge Cato, despite the threat of the militia unit's presence, scorned to answer the question under duress, but the following day he adjourned the court without having conducted any major business. This would seem to have been a minor victory for the northerners, but some grudge against the people involved in that court must still have lingered in the mind of old John Brown.

Meanwhile, the main body of the Pottawatomie Rifles under the younger John Brown remained in the general area where they had first halted. On the afternoon of Sunday the twenty-fifth, an officer of the United States Army found them there and ordered them to disperse. They started home. At their camp that night the elder John Brown and his party rejoined them. By then the main body had heard the story of the massacre; next morning they recognized some of the horses that John Brown, Sr., brought back as those of the murdered settlers. John Brown, Jr., much disturbed, resigned command of the unit and its members chose H. H. Williams in his place.

Returning to the Pottawatomie region, the unit found it in turmoil because of the massacre. Settlers of both parties had joined together in a meeting at which they demanded that the murderers be brought to justice. A number of the innocent members of the Pottawatomie Rifles were arrested immediately upon their return, but eventually all were released except John Brown, Jr., and H. H. Williams, the two commanders of the unit, who were held in prison throughout the summer.

In the meantime, the elder John Brown and his followers, who had separated from the others as they returned, escaped arrest and continued to roam the countryside.

The Battle of Black Jack

Old John Brown and a small group of his men disappeared into a partially settled area in eastern Kansas. On the thirtieth of May, 1856, they were joined by a news correspondent from the East, James Redpath. Redpath was sympathetic to the free-state cause and looked upon John Brown as a hero.

Another free-stater who lived not far from John Brown's camping place was known as "Captain" Shore because he led a small company of armed settlers. He brought provisions to Brown and kept him informed of developments. On May 31 he told Brown that a large group of Missourians were camped at Black Jack Springs on the Santa Fe Trail. Brown and Shore discussed matters and agreed to join forces and move against the Missourians. Their two groups totaled about forty men.

The Missourians, numbering perhaps fifty, were led by Captain H. Clay Pate, who had been made a deputy United States marshal and sent out to arrest Brown. On the morning of June 2, John Brown and his men looked down on Pate's camp from the top of a small roll in the prairie. At a word from Brown his force began to run down the gentle hill toward Pate's group. Shore accompanied them, but his men decided to stay on top of the slope and merely fire at the Missourians — who were all well out of range.

Pate's men scrambled for their weapons and returned the fire. Both groups quickly moved into stream beds to gain some cover. There was then about an eighth of a mile between them. At closer range the fire became more effective. One of Brown's men was shot through the lungs. Another had his nose shot off and the bullet lodged in his shoulder. They were taken from the field. At that point Shore announced that he had had no breakfast and was hungry, and therefore he was going to leave them.

After some maneuvering Brown and his men moved toward the Missourians. Frederick Brown, one of the old man's sons, had been left behind to guard the horses, but he wanted to get into the battle. He had been joined by W. A. Phillips, correspondent for the New York *Tribune*, a strongly abolitionist paper. The two men leaped on horses and came galloping down the Santa Fe Trail, past the positions of the southerners. Brown then called to his father that they had their enemies surrounded.

Captain Pate wanted to talk to Brown and tell him that he had a warrant for his arrest. He sent out a white truce flag; the old man sent the bearer of the flag back to get Pate himself. When Pate arrived on the scene he started to explain his authority to arrest Brown. John Brown cut him off and demanded his immediate surrender while pointing a large revolver at him. Pate had little choice. Some of his men at first refused to give in, but on discovering the plight of their leader they surrendered.

John Brown took twenty-one prisoners. Many of Pate's men had fled during the battle and Brown also let the wounded go. After he had won the battle, old John Brown was quickly joined by other free-staters, including some of those who had disappeared when the shots were flying. The captured southerners were held in camp for three days. Then Colonel Sumner and a body of his cavalry, accompanied by a deputy United States marshal, found the group and ordered Brown to release his captives.

The marshal, named William J. Preston, had warrants for the arrest of a number of the free-staters, but when Sumner told him that he might serve his warrants he looked over the group and announced that he did not recognize any of them. Perhaps he was afraid to make the arrests, but after all he had the cavalry to back him up; perhaps he was a free-state sympathizer. Sumner asked him in disgust what he was there for, told Brown to disperse his group, and then rode away.

Most of Brown's men went home. John Brown and his closest associates disappeared for a time. But a border war had begun.

Move and Counter-Move

At about the same time that Captain Pate's force went looking for John Brown, J. W. Whitfield, the man elected by the proslavery element as the Kansas delegate to the United States Congress, also set out in search of the old man, leading some two hundred and fifty armed Missourians. Colonel Sumner, after freeing Pate and his men and sending them home, encountered Whitfield's considerably larger group and also ordered them to return to Missouri. They agreed to do so, but on the way they pillaged the free-state town of Osawatomie, killing two or three men and carrying away loot from the homes and stores of the town.

On June 5 a group of northerners attacked the southern hamlet of Franklin, a point where proslavery recruits freshly arrived in Kansas were given military training. In the blockhouse they had built, the southerners had a small cannon and the free-staters hoped to capture it. Instead, they were driven off.

The Fourth of July, 1856

Governor Shannon decided that the northern legislature, which met at Topeka, was illegal and must be disbanded. He directed Colonel Sumner, the commanding officer at Fort Leavenworth, to do so the next time the legislature met. It had adjourned on June 13 to meet again at noon on July 4. On June 23 Shannon left Kansas for a time and Daniel Woodson, the proslavery secretary of the territory, became acting governor. Shannon also issued a proclamation forbidding the meeting of the free-state legislature as an act of insurrection.

Sumner, who had arrived outside Topeka and had gone into camp with a body of his troops a couple of days earlier, and who had meanwhile been conferring with the free-staters and advising them not to meet in the face of the governor's orders, rode into town with a force of cavalry and artillery at about noon on the fourth. Two units of the Topeka militia were drawn up outside Constitution Hall, as the legislative building was called, for a Fourth of July ceremony; the ladies of Topeka were presenting them with a flag. The northern leaders, who realized that a showdown with Sumner's United States troops was coming, undoubtedly had placed the militia there with the thought that they might deter Sumner from acting. But when the colonel emplaced his cannon three hundred feet from the building and formed the cavalry on the street in front of it, the militia did not interfere.

Colonel Sumner entered the hall and was invited to the speaker's platform. After the roll was called, he rose. Pointing out that he had recently come back from the border, where he had been sending home companies of Missourians, he announced that he was there under federal authority to disband this body. "I now command you to disperse." A free-stater asked if Sumner would drive them out at bayonet point and he replied that he would use whatever force was necessary. He and Marshal Donalson then went to the senate chamber. The senate had not yet convened and Donalson announced that the senators would be arrested if they did so. None of them challenged him.

Growing Violence

Throughout the summer of 1856, James H. Lane, the most militant of the northern party leaders, had been touring the states of the North raising money and enlisting settlers. He was an oratorical spellbinder and he gave his speech the title, "Bleeding Kansas." The meeting that he ad-

A portrait of James H. Lane, the powerful antislavery leader, who was known as the Grim Chieftain of Kansas. (Kansas State Historical Society, Topeka)

dressed in Chicago alone promised to send five hundred settlers and maintain them in Kansas for a year. Lane and other speakers from Kansas stirred up a great deal of sentiment in the northern states. Soon a national organization was formed to support the free-state cause in Kansas.

Because Missouri stood across the normal routes of approach to Kansas, the southerners were at first able to blunt this northern effort. They guarded all the roads and river crossings and boarded all the steamboats. They searched the belongings of any settlers coming in from the North and if they found a weapon they confiscated it and forced the would-be settler who had owned it to go back. On one occasion the captain of a river steamer tipped off the Missourians that one of his Kansas-bound passengers, D. S. Hoyt of Massachusetts, had in the hold of the vessel one hundred Sharps rifles, four breech-loading cannon, and a quantity of ammunition. A mob boarded the steamer at the first landing place and threatened to lynch Hoyt, but he refused to sign over the arms as they demanded. Finally the Missourians took his shipment anyway but left Hoyt unharmed. He thereupon returned to St. Louis and by legal action forced the steamboat line to pay for the weapons that the officers of the boat had surrendered to the mob.

Soon the National Kansas Committee, as the northern organization was called, decided to open a road through Iowa and Nebraska, thus allowing settlers to reach the northern boundary of Kansas without passing through Missouri. The road became known as the Lane Trail.

Early in August several companies of immigrants who had come over the Lane Trail gathered on the northern border of Kansas. They totaled about four hundred armed men, and the theatrical Lane, who liked to wear knee boots, a red sash, a cloak, and a military cap, was their leader. "Lane's Army of the North," as the group was called, seemed poised for an invasion. But some of the less aggressive northerners persuaded Lane to give up his command and he hurried on to Lawrence. His men came across the border in small groups, moved peaceably to various places in the territory, and took up claims. Their arrival caused no incidents, but their numbers reinforced the northerners' fighting strength.

Lane's return to Kansas Territory was the signal for a burst of free-state guerrilla activity. On August 5, an Illinois company led by a man named Brown (no relative of John Brown) attacked a Georgia colony of about two hundred people. As the northerners approached, the settlers from Georgia fled. Brown and his men destroyed a blockhouse that the Georgians had built, took all the provisions and belongings left behind, and burned the homes.

Lane himself headed a force that attacked the southern town of Franklin on August 12. The defenders took refuge in their log blockhouse. After a considerable exchange of shots, Lane's men loaded a wagon with hay, set it afire, and backed it up to the building. As the logs caught fire the southerners were forced out of their stronghold. The northerners captured fourteen prisoners and wounded three, one of whom later died; one free-stater was killed and six wounded. The rest of the defenders retreated to another southern base a little distance away that was manned by a Georgia company. It was called Fort Saunders. (These little villages were called forts simply because each of them contained a log blockhouse for defense.) At Franklin the northerners captured a number of arms including the cannon they had coveted.

D. S. Hoyt, the man whose shipment of weapons was taken by force from the Missouri River steamboat, had gone from Lawrence to Fort Saunders on the eleventh to try to negotiate a settlement with the men there. On his way back to Lawrence he was murdered, and the free-staters were sure that he had been followed by some of the men in the fort and killed by them. On August 15 Lane attacked Fort Saunders. Hoyt's body had just been found and the northerners were enraged; they charged the fort, only to find that its defenders had fled, even leaving behind them a hot meal on the table. The dramatic Lane forbade his men to eat it because it might be poisoned. The northerners burned the place.

Lane then turned over the command of a column to Captain Samuel Walker who went on to attack Fort Titus, another southern position. The fort was, in reality, a settlement named for its leader, Colonel Henry T. Titus, whose home stood in the middle. The northerners trained the cannon on his home and attacked at dawn. After half an hour of brisk fighting, the defenders gave up. Titus was seriously wounded. He and nineteen others were taken prisoner. One of the northern leaders, a Captain Shombre who had just arrived from Indiana, was wounded during the battle and died the next day.

The southern prisoners were taken back to Lawrence. Governor Shannon visited the town on August 17 and negotiated an agreement that the prisoners would be freed in return for a group of free-state prisoners being held by the southerners and the cannon that Sheriff Jones had taken from Lawrence. This agreement gave northerners both pieces of artillery.

By this time Governor Shannon had reached a state of complete despair. He was threatened and despised by both sides and all of his attempts to control the situation came to nothing. On August 21 he resigned. Until a new governor was appointed, proslavery Secretary Daniel Woodson again became the acting governor. On August 25 Woodson proclaimed the territory to be in a state of insurrection and called out the militia. Once again Missourians streamed across the border to fight in Kansas.

The Battle of Osawatomie

On August 25, the day of Woodson's proclamation, about one hundred and fifty Missourians camped nine miles south of the northern settlement of Osawatomie. The northerners assembled to meet them, and a body of over one hundred men attacked the southern camp at noon on the twenty-sixth. After about ten minutes the Missourians broke ranks and fled.

The John Brown cabin at Osawatomie. It is preserved today on the 23-acre John Brown Memorial Park grounds. (Photo by Cushing)

The Missouri invasion was not to be put down so easily, however. By the twenty-ninth some twelve hundred Missourians had gone into camp on the Santa Fe Trail seven or eight miles east of Black Jack Springs, where John Brown had captured Captain Pate. Senator Atchison was with them. Another southern leader, John W. Reid, a member of the Missouri legislature, was sent out that night with about three hundred men to destroy Osawatomie.

Early the next morning Frederick Brown, one of the sons of old John Brown who had taken part in the massacre with his father, set out from Osawatomie, where he had been visiting an uncle, to ride to Lawrence. As he started away he met a scouting party of Missourians led by the Reverend Martin White. In the darkness he could not see them clearly, but supposed that they were friends. "Good morning, boys," he said. There was no answer. "I believe I know you," he continued. White said, "I know *you*," and shot him in the chest. He died immediately.

Later that morning Brown's uncle and a friend discovered the body. At that time another element of the scouting party appeared, riding toward them. The uncle went a little distance off the road and lay down in some bushes, but the younger man ran away on foot over the bare prairie, and the Missourians galloped after him. He ran by a settler's cabin and his pursuers, seeing a man there, shot him in the face as they rode past. The young fugitive periodically turned and fired at the horsemen, but they soon rode up to him and killed him.

Meanwhile, the alarmed town sent out messages to a small guerrilla force commanded by John Brown that was camped a little distance to the north. Brown and thirty men set out for Osawatomie. Not long after sunrise they went into a defensive position south of the town in a line of bushes that grew along a break in the ground, near a river. From there they fired on the main body of the advancing southerners, but it soon

[45]

became apparent that thirty men could not stop three hundred. As Reid's force opened fire with a cannon loaded with grapeshot (the equivalent of a giant shotgun), Brown's men were forced back. Old John Brown had put his defensive position on the wrong side of the river; now he and his men had to retreat across the stream under fire. One of his northerners hid between saw logs that were floating in the water and from there shot and wounded a Missourian, but another northerner was killed while trying to wade across. Several of Brown's party were captured. John Brown, his son Jason, and a few of the others got across and escaped.

Having defeated John Brown's force, Reid's men pushed on to the town. There they robbed the homes and stores and set fire to them. One citizen was beaten to death with a spirit level, which was left on the ground beside his crushed head. Reid, in a report of the raid, said that thirty northerners were killed and that "the boys would burn the town to the ground. I could not help it." Afterward, at their camp site, the Missourians tried one of John Brown's men whom they had captured. This man, Charles Keiser, had left Missouri to settle in Kansas. They found him guilty of treason to Missouri; he was not present at the trial, but after he was found guilty a guard went and got him, he was marched a little distance from camp, and was executed by a firing squad.

On the thirty-first, James H. Lane finally arrived on the scene with about three hundred northerners. In the meantime, all of the Missourians except Reid's forces had scattered, and Atchison had returned to Missouri with some of his staff while others ranged through Kansas. Lane came up with Reid's command and attacked. The southerners' marksmanship was poor and they did not respond well to the orders of their officers; apparently they had been celebrating the looting of Osawatomie with some heavy drinking and were not in the best condition for a fight. They held off the northern force until darkness fell, but then they quietly pulled back and headed for Missouri.

Continued Strife

While Lane was moving against Reid's force, Marshal Donalson and some territorial militia were scouring the country west of Lawrence in search of free-staters for whom the marshal had warrants. Donalson arrested a number of northerners and the militia burned seven homes and plundered others. Taking their prisoners with them, they then headed back to the southern town of Lecompton.

Lane, hearing of this move, took his command toward Lecompton in two columns, one along each side of the Kansas River. As they approached the town, a number of the militia there, including several high-ranking officers, decided that it was time for them to go home. Acting Governor Woodson suddenly found that he had no men to defend the town. He turned once more to the United States troops at Fort Leavenworth. Colonel Sumner had recently been transferred and Colonel P. St. G. Cooke had assumed command of the troops. Cooke sent a message to the proslavery men suggesting that it would be helpful if they released their prisoners, and then he rode out with a body of cavalry to intercept Lane and his forces. Shortly before Cooke met the northerners he received a message that the prisoners were being freed. Lane and his men were somewhat mollified when they heard this news and they had no desire to start a battle with the regular troops, so they went back to Lawrence.

In the town of Leavenworth, an election had been held on September 1, 1856, and a proslavery man named Murphy had become mayor. He ordered that every free-state family be expelled from town. His men broke into houses and stores and drove out the occupants. One northerner, who had previously been tarred and feathered by a mob, shot and killed two of Murphy's men as they approached, and was himself promptly killed. Several hundred Missourians paraded the streets rounding up anyone they suspected of being sympathetic to the northern cause. About one hundred and fifty men, women, and children were herded aboard a moored river boat that was converted into a prison. Others who attempted to board vessels traveling downstream were shot; some escaped as far as Missouri and were then arrested and sent back. Refugees from Leavenworth fled to Lawrence and other free-state towns.

The northerners at Lawrence decided to attack Leavenworth, but they sent only a small detachment. On the eleventh of September that group met a small group of southerners whom they defeated and captured; then, instead of going on to Leavenworth they returned to Lawrence. At about the same time Lane, with thirty of his own men and fifty more from Topeka, attacked a southern guerrilla band that had been harassing settlers in the area northwest of Lawrence, that had burned one village, and that had then gone into a defensive position in a strongly fortified place called Hickory Point (this was not the place where Charles Dow had been murdered, but another of the same name). Lane marched to Hickory Point, but upon discovering just how strong the southern position was, he sent off to Lawrence for more men and a cannon. The ensuing Battle of Hickory Point lasted several hours; one southerner was killed and four wounded while five northerners were wounded. The northerners won.

Old print depicts the town of Leavenworth as it looked in the mid-1850's. (Kansas State Historical Society, Topeka)

Governor Geary

John W. Geary was appointed the third governor of Kansas Territory on July 31, 1856. Geary was a stronger man than his predecessors. He had attained the rank of colonel during the Mexican War and when Mexico City was captured he was made its commandant. He had been the first mayor of San Francisco and had helped to establish the government of California.

Soon after his arrival in Kansas on September 9, Geary issued a proclamation disbanding the militia called up by Woodson, but on September 13 yet another invasion began from Missouri. Once more Lawrence was the target of the invaders, who were accompanied by Atchison, Reid, and other proslavery leaders. Geary, accompanied by Colonel Cooke, three hundred United States soldiers, and four cannon, arrived at Lawrence on the fourteenth and Cooke set up a defense of the place. By the fifteenth Lawrence was under siege by twenty-five hundred Missourians. Geary rode out to meet them.

The governor ordered the Missourians' camp to disband. A firm territorial governor was something new, and at first the southerners were surprised. Some of them were willing to leave immediately, but the firebrands among them announced that they were going to fight the United States troops on the spot. After a good deal of muttering, however, the invading force turned around and went back to Missouri.

James H. Lane had conveniently retired to Nebraska, but he had left a body of about one hundred men carrying out guerrilla operations near Hickory Point. Colonel Cooke's soldiers found them on the fifteenth and arrested them. A number of them were subsequently given penitentiary sentences. For the time there were no more irregular military operations in Kansas.

But Geary was not able to control the political and judicial problems of the territory. As one example, a small band of the southerners who had been dispersed at Lawrence found, on their way home, a lame man plowing in a field. They took his horse and when he objected, one of them, Charles Hays, shot him. A little later Geary, accompanied by the proslavery Judge Cato, rode by and found the wounded man. At Geary's direction, Cato took his dying statement. The governor had a warrant issued for the murderer, whose name at that time was unknown. None of the federal officials would make any move to discover the name of the murderer; all of them were southern sympathizers. Geary than had his own investigators gather the evidence and arrest the man. A grand jury indicted Charles Hays for murder in the first degree. Another proslavery magistrate, Judge Lecompte, immediately released him on bail, accepting Sheriff Jones as bondsman. The governor had Hays rearrested. Lecompte again freed him.

National politics further complicated the Kansas situation. In 1856 James Buchanan, a Democrat, was elected president. He denounced the Topeka government. The Law and Order party, as the Kansas proslavery men called themselves, decided that the time was ripe to make the territory once and for all a slave area. Geary recommended to the proslavery territorial legislature, then meeting at Lecompton, the repeal of restrictive and proslavery laws, but with a few minor exceptions they made no changes. Instead, the southerners laid plans for another constitutional convention that would be rigged in such a way that the proslavery group was certain to win. Geary protested the plans, but the legislature ignored him.

The Law and Order party changed its name to the National Democratic party of Kansas. Governor Geary was a Democrat, but his attempts to stabilize the political situation in Kansas won him no friends among the southern group. In fact, on several occasions they even threatened to assassinate him. In one incident, a disreputable man whom Geary had re-

James Buchanan, 15th president of the United States.
(Library of Congress)

fused to confirm as a replacement for Sheriff Jones, who recently had resigned, waylaid the governor and spat in his face. The man had stationed other thugs nearby, hoping that he could start a fight with the governor and then call in the others to beat him up or kill him. Geary ignored the insult and walked on past.

By March 4, 1857, the governor had had enough; he was receiving no backing from the federal government in his attempts to bring order, and he resigned. President Buchanan had his replacement waiting. He was a Mississippi lawyer and politician named Robert J. Walker.

[51]

Victory for the Free-Staters

Governor Walker took a moderate approach. He pointed out what had been obvious all along: climatic conditions in Kansas would never support slavery. It was economically feasible to use slave labor only in a climate where large numbers of slaves could easily be sustained throughout the winter, where large areas of land could be worked during most of the year, and especially where the kind of crops could be grown that slaves could till. The fierce Kansas winters permitted none of these things. But the moderate Walker soon found himself attacked by both sides: He was not southern enough for the southerners and much too southern for the northerners. Even President Buchanan failed to support him.

On June 15, 1857, the election was held for delegates to a constitutional convention. By gerrymandering (rearranging election districts) and failure to register voters in free-state areas (in fifteen counties there was no registration at all), the southern forces carried the day. The constitutional convention met at Lecompton on September 7, appointed committees, and adjourned until October 19.

On October 5 there was an election for a new territorial legislature and delegate to the United States Congress. This time the free-staters decided to vote. As a result their candidate for Congress won. The southerners appeared to have carried the legislature, but then it developed that once again there had been massive election frauds. Governor Walker directed that the false ballots be thrown out, and the free-staters were then in control of the legislature as well.

The southern-dominated convention gathered again at Lecompton on the nineteenth in full realization that Kansas had, in its first truly representative election, declared itself for the North. The southerners, however, arrived at a formula that would retain their proslavery constitution.

[52]

They would permit the voters to decide whether they wanted the constitution "with" or "without" slavery — but "without" meant only that no more slaves could be brought into Kansas. Slavery would still be legal; the voters could not decide upon the constitution itself. Very few slaves had been taken into the territory, but this southern move outraged the northerners, who as a matter of principle wanted to outlaw slavery.

The free-staters managed to call the new territorial legislature into session. It was now controlled by the northern faction and it quickly decided upon a territory-wide referendum on the whole constitution, to be held on January 4, 1858. Meanwhile, the southern-controlled constitutional convention held the election for the constitution; the free-staters boycotted it and the constitution was voted in "with" slavery. Three weeks later the referendum was held. This time the proslavery men refrained from voting and the constitution was defeated.

In the meantime another governor, James W. Denver, arrived on the scene, but he had little influence on developments. President Buchanan sent the proslavery constitution to the United States Congress for ratification. There it precipitated a lengthy political battle; as a final compromise it was sent back to the people of Kansas for another vote. They defeated it resoundingly. Kansas was definitely in the northern camp.

The Marais des Cygnes Massacre

While Congress was arguing over the Kansas constitution there was yet another bloody episode in the territory.

On May 19, 1858, a pleasant spring day, a group of about thirty Missourians came into Kansas. They were led by Charles A. Hamelton, a former Kansas settler who had been forced to leave his claim and flee to Missouri. They crossed the Marais des Cygnes River at a settlement called Trading Post and made prisoners of the men they found there. Soon afterward, however, they freed all but one, John F. Campbell, whom they forced to accompany them.

While moving along the road they met three other men and made them prisoners. Then they went from claim to nearby claim, rounding up six more settlers whom they drove ahead of them down the road. Finally, they added to their collection a man they met who was driving a yoke of oxen.

In time they came to a blacksmith shop operated by a settler named Ely Snyder, a strong free-state man. Halting their prisoners a little distance away, most of Hamelton's band went to capture Snyder. Hamelton and half a dozen of his men stood looking down on the shop from a small hill while three men went down and called to the owner to come out. Snyder stepped to the door, took one look at the men on the hill, and jumped back into the shop. As he turned to get his shotgun he found that another of the raiders had come in behind him and was in his way. He hit the raider so hard that he knocked him completely out of the shop.

Snyder fired a load of buckshot at one of the men who was going back up the hill. Then he moved behind a nearby stone wall, from where he traded shots with the marauders. Snyder's wife and daughter were washing laundry nearby; the girl went to get her brother and he came on the run, shooting as he did so. The Missourians were already retreating.

Hamelton was frustrated and angry at being driven off by the Snyders. He returned to the place where he had left his prisoners and made them form a line in a narrow ravine. He divided his party, putting half of it on each side of the ravine and ordering his men to shoot down at the prisoners below them. One of Hamelton's guerrillas rebelled and galloped away, saying that he would have no part in an act of this sort. Hamelton prevailed with the others, however, and they fired on the defenseless men below.

Etching shows the massacre at the Marais des Cygnes River on May 19, 1858. (Kansas State Historical Society, Topeka)

Many of the Missourians at that point wheeled and rode away, overcome by what they had done. But a few remained with Hamelton, and they went down to examine the bodies to make sure that they were dead. The remaining raiders must also have been somewhat shaken, for although five of the victims were dead, five others were only wounded and one had not been hit at all but was feigning death. One wounded man whom they saw breathing they shot in the mouth, but they did not realize that the others were still alive. They took whatever valuables they could find on the bodies and left.

The Killing of Gaius Jenkins

The Free-State party itself was having troubles. There was a major split between the radical element led by James H. Lane and the conservatives led by Charles Robinson. The split was further widened when Lane killed a friend of Robinson's, a settler named Gaius Jenkins.

Jenkins and Lane each had his house upon the same claim, located about half a mile from the Free State Hotel in Lawrence. The houses were three hundred yards apart. Lane had lived with Jenkins for a year, then moved to the other house and brought his wife and four children there from Indiana. Jenkins believed that the claim was his. Lane said that Jenkins had simply been his tenant, and that the claim was his.

The argument between these two men came to focus on a well that was in Lane's yard. Jenkins was used to going to the well for water. The path that he followed, however, led through Lane's new vegetable garden. Lane nailed up the back gate in Jenkins's fence and asked Jenkins to go around and use the front gate, about one hundred and fifty feet away.

After increasing friction, during which Jenkins broke down the gate and Lane nailed it up again several times, the matter came to a head on June 3, 1858. That afternoon Jenkins found the gate nailed shut again. He took an ax to it and despite warnings from Lane that he would shoot if they came through the gate, Jenkins went through, toward the well. His hired man followed, with a pistol in his belt. Two other male members of Jenkins' family remained in his yard, one of them with a loaded Sharps rifle.

Jenkins had thrown aside the ax and was unarmed. In his excitement, the hired man had thrown aside the two water pails that he started out with. Lane retreated to his house and then came out again with a shotgun. He stationed himself in front of Jenkins and told Jenkins that if he moved another step he would fire. Jenkins continued to walk ahead; Lane fired; Jenkins fell, struck in the chest and abdomen by a load of buck-shot, and died within fifteen minutes. The hired man fired the pistol at Lane and an unidentified person fired the Sharps rifle at him, wounding him. He went back to his house.

On June 15 Lane was brought to trial for murder. He was still weak from his wounds. The arguments centered on whether or not Lane was entitled to defend his holdings against armed and aggressive trespass. The trial lasted until June 30, when the judge announced that Lane was discharged because there was no proof that he had committed the crime of "willful murder" as defined by Kansas law.

The Thirty-Ninth State

The killing of Jenkins was the death blow of the Free-State party, which already was beginning to fall apart. There was no longer room in it for Lane, so he spearheaded the formation of the new Republican party in Kansas. Most Free-Staters became Republicans, though a few moved over to the Democrats. Even Charles Robinson in time joined the Republican party. Delegates were elected in June of 1859 for a new convention that would draw up a constitution for the state of Kansas. The Republicans won handily, but they still claimed that the Democrats had imported votes from Missouri.

This convention was dominated by the northern element that hated slavery, and its actions showed how the northerners really felt. It of course banned slavery in the new state, but it specified that voters must be white. Only after some argument were Negroes permitted to enter schools, and a move was even made to prohibit any free Negroes from coming into the state, but that suggestion was tabled.

The northerners also took the opportunity to gerrymander the dis-

The Great Seal of the State of Kansas which achieved statehood on January 29, 1861. Latin motto means "To the stars through difficulties." (Photo by Cushing)

tricts to nullify Democratic voting strength. They engaged in a lengthy discussion of the boundaries of the future state and of the location of the new state capital. Topeka was chosen capital and those who supported other towns immediately charged corruption and bribery.

Kansas did not become the thirty-ninth state until after the national election of 1860. When Abraham Lincoln and the Republicans won that election there was little difficulty in making Kansas a state. Buchanan signed the bill on January 29, 1861. The first governor of the state was Charles Robinson, and one of the first senators was James H. Lane.

War Comes Officially

Almost immediately upon the official declaration of the Civil War, Kansas provided six hundred and fifty men to the Union. By the end of the war, about twenty thousand men had signed up out of the thirty thousand in the eighteen to forty-five age bracket who were residents of the new state. The overwhelming response to the call to arms was probably one result of the fact that events of the past several years had drawn adventurous men into Kansas in far greater numbers than men who truly wanted to carve farms out of the new lands.

Much of the fighting in the West was in Missouri and other surrounding states; only occasionally did it overlap into Kansas. But many of the Kansans who joined the army went to fight in Missouri, and many of them took the opportunity to settle old scores.

Senator James H. Lane was made a brigadier general, and he set to work to recruit his brigade along the Kansas border. Its major elements were the Third and Fourth Kansas Volunteer Infantry and the Fifth Kansas Cavalry. Many of the members were former guerrillas who had fought for Lane. In Missouri, at that time, the Confederate general, Sterling Price, was fighting a small Union force commanded by Colonel James A. Mulligan. But because Lane made no move to help Mulligan, he was defeated by Price. Lane had decided to follow behind Price's army and punish any Missourians who had helped the Confederates. He ordered that "everything disloyal, from a Shanghai rooster to a Durham cow, must be cleaned out," and his men set out to do just that.

As Lane's brigade passed into Missouri, every home in its way was looted. None were spared. Loyal families whose men were serving in the Union army suffered as much as those who backed the Confederacy. Livestock, furniture, and jewelry were taken from all. Arriving at the small town of Osceola, where Price had had his headquarters, Lane found some military supplies in a warehouse and decided that he would destroy the town. Nine men were court-martialed and shot. The teams and wagons of the inhabitants were loaded with all the movable property Lane's men could plunder and were driven away. Then all but three buildings were set on fire. One of the buildings that was destroyed was the county courthouse with all of its records. "The Grim Chieftain of Kansas," as Lane was beginning to be known, led his men back toward the border, burning houses as he went. When they arrived at Lawrence they divided their wagons full of loot.

Jayhawkers

A number of lesser guerrilla chiefs were leading Kansans in raids through Missouri at the same time. Next to Lane, the most notorious was Doc Jennison. Jennison had grown up in Wisconsin, where he had been educated as a physician and had practiced medicine, then had moved to Kansas and joined the free-state ranks. His first fame was earned in 1860 when he hanged two Missourians who had come into Kansas to hunt runaway slaves. Early in 1861 he was made captain of an irregular band that moved into Missouri on a raiding and looting expedition and was promptly ordered back to Kansas by the United States Army commander in the area.

In July, Jennison's group once again crossed into Missouri and acted as advance guard for a Kansas force moving against the town of Harrisonville, where southern troops were reported to be gathering. His men were the first to reach the town and they found no enemy soldiers, but by the time the main body had arrived they had broken into most of the

Guerrilla chieftain Charles R. ("Doc") Jennison. (Kansas State Historical Society, Topeka)

stores and homes and looted them. They also took all the money they could find, including that of the county government. Many of those they robbed were strong pro-Union men such as Colonel Henry Younger, who lost several thousand dollars' worth of horses and carriages. (Younger's sons, Coleman and James, would later become noted outlaws along the frontier.)

As the result of this and similar raids, good horses of questionable ownership that were offered for sale in Iowa and Illinois came to be given the joking pedigree, "out of Missouri by Jennison." Even so, Jennison was authorized to raise a regiment of volunteer cavalry in Kansas for the United States service. This was the Seventh Kansas Cavalry, which came to be known as "Jennison's Jayhawkers." (Jayhawker was the name given northern guerrillas operating along the Kansas-Missouri border. The reason for the name is uncertain.) Thus his operations were given some respectability.

In November and December of 1861 Jennison made his base in Jackson County, Missouri, where his Jayhawkers enjoyed full opportunities for loot and murder. Any Missourian was fair game, whether his sympathies were with the North or South. General Halleck, who commanded the United States Department of Missouri, wrote in December, "The conduct of the forces under Lane and Jennison has done more for the enemy in this state than could have been accomplished by twenty thousand of his own army." Halleck ordered the United States forces under his command to drive Jennison's regiment and Lane's brigade (which was again foraging in Missouri) back into Kansas.

The Reaction

The lawless border-ruffian element in Missouri had had at least as much experience as the Jayhawkers in guerrilla fighting, but it had never had the backing of a large number of Missourians. Now, many respectable men were swept into guerrilla warfare. Southern sympathizers who were unable to join the Confederate army or preferred less regular discipline, as well as former Union sympathizers who had been turned against the North by Jayhawker atrocities, joined with the more practical outlaws who were interested mainly in crime. There was a scattering of unstable fanatics, just as there was on the other side. The result of this mixture was a burst of spontaneous prosouthern guerrilla activity. Armed bands not only fought the Jayhawkers but also conducted their own raids into Kansas.

The most famous of the prosouthern guerrilla bands was the one directed by William Quantrill, an Ohioan who was only twenty-four years old when the Civil War began and who was to die of his wounds after

Two portraits of the famed proslavery guerrilla leader William Quantrill. At right he appears in Confederate officer's uniform. (Left, Photo by Cushing; Right, Kansas State Historical Society, Topeka)

a fight in Kentucky at the age of twenty-seven. Tall, slender, with an almost pretty face and auburn hair, the only outer sign of his character was the cold blue of his eyes. When he was nineteen he moved to Kansas, where he lived in several places including Lawrence. By 1859 he had become a teacher in a small rural school near the free-state town of Osawatomie. Then he was suspected of stealing a horse, so he moved to Missouri in December of 1860. He did this, however, in a manner that set the pattern for his later vicious dealings.

[63]

Five young abolitionists from Lawrence were going on a raid into Missouri to free some slaves. These men were Quakers, but they armed themselves with pistols and bowie knives. Quantrill joined them and to some degree even became their leader. As they approached the farm of a rich Missouri planter, Quantrill went on ahead to scout out the ground, or so he told his companions. Actually he went to the planter's farm, warned the men there of the raid, telling them it was to be led by Jim Montgomery, another notorious Jayhawker, and helped them to arrange an ambush for the raiding party. He then returned to his comrades and after dark led them to the farmhouse; he went to the door, supposedly to demand the release of the slaves. No sooner was he let in than the men stationed to one side of the house fired on the unsuspecting Quakers using shotguns loaded with buckshot. One Quaker was killed, two were wounded, and two were unharmed. One of the wounded men and one of the unwounded escaped and eventually returned to Lawrence. The other unwounded man carried away under fire the most seriously injured, taking refuge in a woods not far away, but the two were later hunted down by Quantrill.

By 1862 Quantrill had surrounded himself with a group of young men who were quite willing to follow someone who combined as much intelligence, cold-bloodedness, and daring as he did. They devoted themselves to attacking small bands of Jayhawkers in Missouri and to making their own raids on the Kansas towns along the border, where they in turn burned, looted, and murdered. The more extensive the violence of the Kansas guerrillas became, the larger became the numbers of Missourians who decided that their only answer was to become guerrillas themselves. By 1863 Quantrill had made a trip to Richmond, Virginia, the Confederate capital, and returned with a commission as a captain of rangers. He thereupon began to call himself "colonel" and on occasion wore the uniform of a Confederate colonel.

[64]

The Banishing of the Women

In the course of the operations along the border, United States forces arrested a number of women who were accused of acting as spies or otherwise helping the Confederates. These female prisoners were quartered under guard in several buildings in Kansas City. One building, in which eleven of the women were housed, was an old, three-story brick structure. All eleven of the prisoners were relatives of some of Quantrill's men.

The building was structurally weak. The officer commanding the guard, a lieutenant of the Ninth Kansas Regiment, on the morning of August 14 reported that the walls had cracked and that he believed the place no longer was safe. A staff officer came to investigate and decided that there was no danger. But in the early afternoon the lieutenant, who was still uneasy about the building, told one of the men of his company who had some construction experience to check its condition. As the man was on the top floor, looking it over, the walls slowly began to separate from the ceiling. He called to the guard to get the women out and they all ran for their lives.

The building collapsed in a tremendous cloud of dust. Four women were dead in the ruins and others were injured. The unhurt women immediately started to berate the Union soldiers for undermining the building and making it fall down, and word quickly ran through the gathering crowd that that was what had happened. The crowd became so antagonistic to the soldiers that the guards had to fix bayonets and force some of the bystanders to help rescue the wounded and bring out the dead.

There was no evidence that the troops had undermined the building and the charge was absurd on the face of it, but the story was widely believed. To counteract it, the Union authorities circulated an even more absurd story, that the women had been trying to dig a tunnel out of the building and had brought it down on top of themselves. No one believed this tale and in the minds of many people its publication confirmed the other story. Among those who felt certain that Kansas troops had killed their women were the men of Quantrill's band.

Four days later General Thomas Ewing, who commanded United States forces in the border district, issued an order that made good sense from the military point of view, but that was not good psychology at that particular time: "The wives and children of known guerrillas, and also women who are heads of families and are willfully engaged in aiding guerrillas, will be notified . . . to remove out of this district and out of the State of Missouri forthwith." In other words, the wives, sweethearts, and sisters of the southern guerrillas were to be deported.

Quantrill's Raid on Lawrence

The guerrillas reacted violently. They thought that the Union forces had deliberately killed some of their women, and now it was evident that they were going to drive out the rest of them. As one guerrilla said, "We could stand no more." Quantrill channeled this reaction to his own ends. For some while he had been planning a raid on Lawrence; now the time had come. Of course a raid on the civilians of Lawrence in retaliation for the actions of the United States Army commander in Kansas City followed absolutely no logic, but Lawrence was a symbol of everything the Missourians hated and the thought of such a raid gave them an outlet for their boiling emotions.

On August 19, about three hundred guerrillas started toward Lawrence. On their way they were joined by Colonel John Holt, a real Con-

[66]

federate colonel, who had about one hundred Confederate army recruits. Holt had owned a hardware store in Missouri, had been burned out by Jennison, and had then joined the Confederate army. He had been recruiting in northern Missouri and on his way back fell in with Quantrill. As other small bands joined them, Quantrill's force grew to about four hundred and fifty men. At three o'clock on the afternoon of the twentieth they crossed into Kansas. Captain J. A. Pike of the Ninth Kansas Volunteers commanded a small Union post pearby. He noted the size of the raiding party and made no effort to stop them. His only action was to send a message to another small post twelve miles away; the commander of that post joined Pike and with a combined force of some two hundred men they set out about midnight to follow the invaders, nine hours too late.

Quantrill's horsemen marched in columns of fours. As they galloped along they forced settlers to guide them over the roads and trails. As soon as a guide no longer knew the road they shot him. One settler along the way had once had one of the guerrillas arrested; that guerrilla paused long enough to beat the man to death with a musket. On Friday, the twenty-first, at the dawn of a clear, hot day, Quantrill's men halted a little distance out of Lawrence. Most of the two thousand townspeople were still asleep. Quantrill sent in a scouting party while he organized his Missourians into groups of forty-five or fifty men and gave each an assigned mission; he had, after all, lived in the town for some time and knew it well. Before the scouts could come back to report that there were no defenders, the main body of the guerrillas charged in.

The first man killed was a Negro minister who had been appointed a lieutenant in the Second Colored Regiment. He was shot while milking his cow. Once in the city, the guerrillas broke into smaller groups to carry out their assigned jobs. Quantrill, with one such group, galloped to the Eldridge House hotel, firing to right and left as they went.

In Lawrence there were two camps for Union army recruits, one for those of the Second Colored Regiment and one for those of the Four-teenth Kansas Cavalry. These were the first targets of the guerrillas. Neither camp of young teen-agers had had much training and neither was armed. Most of them were still asleep when the guerrillas rode over them, shooting and trampling them as they lay in their tents. One raider took the United States flag that had flown over one of the camps, tied it to the tail of his horse, and rode away in search of other victims.

Quantrill pulled up in front of the Eldridge House, a four-story brick building that the raiders thought might be used as a fort. While they were halted there in some indecision, a gong was sounded inside. Its purpose was to wake the sleeping guests, but the guerrillas decided that it was a warning signal and they fell back across the street. A Captain Alexander Banks, who was provost marshal of Kansas, was staying at the hotel. He awoke to find the street outside full of milling guerrillas who were shooting at random. Probably because of their stunned surprise, few people in Lawrence made any attempt to defend themselves. Banks, after a brief consultation with some of the other men, hung a white sheet out of a window.

Quantrill moved forward. He rode on a fine captured horse and in his belt were four pistols. He called up to ask if the white flag meant that the hotel had surrendered. Banks said that it did if he would guarantee the safety of his prisoners. A loud cheer went up from the guerrillas. Quantrill and a few of his men entered the hotel and he announced that it was to be burned. On the preceding evening there had been a meeting in Lawrence to organize the Kansas Pacific Railroad and as a result the hotel was packed with people, many of them comparatively well-to-do. They were like chickens for the guerrillas' plucking and Quantrill's men set to work robbing them methodically, taking money and jewelry from both men and women.

Throughout the small city loot and murder were the order of the

[68]

An action sketch of Quantrill's raid on Lawrence, Kansas, in August, 1863. (Kansas State Historical Society, Topeka)

day. Among the first establishments looted were the saloons, and from then on many of the guerrillas, who were irresponsible under any conditions, were also drunk. Leaders of the small raiding groups carried lists of men who were to be executed, but they did not confine their murders to their lists. Citizens were dragged from their houses and killed, or shot as they ran from buildings that were burned down around them. Bearded men on horseback galloped after any male pedestrians they saw, riding them down and killing them. At one hotel, the Johnson House, the guerrillas brought out twelve men, lined them up, and shot them with pistols. Another group of raiders grabbed two wounded men and threw them into the flames of a burning building. Amazingly, there were few attempts at defense by the men of Lawrence; in the few cases where there were, the guerrillas usually went away and left the defenders alone. Colonel Holt of the Confederate army saved a number of men from death, but he was one of the few raiders who showed any humanity.

One aim of the raid was to capture Senator James H. Lane and take him back to Missouri for public hanging. (Lane had not remained a general for long; he had discovered that by law he could not be a general and a senator at the same time, and he had decided to keep the more powerful job.) The senator was asleep in his new house when he was awakened by the noise of the raid and quickly realized what was happening. He jumped from his bed, ran to the front door, and wrenched off the brass nameplate. Barefoot, and still wearing only his nightshirt, he dashed through his house and ran out into a nearby cornfield. From there, the tall, thin Lane made his way to a farmhouse where he borrowed a pair of trousers from a short, fat man, an old straw hat, and some old boots. From another farmer he received a plow horse but no saddle. Bareback, he rode away quickly — as he later explained, to get help.

Meanwhile Mrs. Lane had to contend with the guerrillas, who proceeded to ransack the house and then burn it. She begged them to help

Mrs. James H. Lane, wife of the senator, who survived the bloody raid on Lawrence. (Kansas State Historical Society, Topeka)

How Lawrence looked after Quantrill's raid. (Kansas State Historical Society, Topeka)

her save her piano, and in the irrational way of people under stress they agreed to do so. But some were drunk and all were impatient, and after struggling with the instrument for a short time they left it to the flames.

A few people who had befriended Quantrill when he was a lonely young unknown in Lawrence were spared his wrath. The owner of the City Hotel had once done him a favor and so that hotel was not burned.

A woman who had nursed him when he was ill was robbed of a ring by one of the raiders; she complained to Quantrill and he saw that it was returned. The house of former Governor Robinson (who had served only one term and had then been deposed by the militant Republicans, in part because he tried to restrain Lane and the other Jayhawkers) was not burned or looted; this immediate good fortune, however, turned out in the long run to be bad luck, for Robinson's political opponents implied that it was the result of treasonable dealings with the enemy.

At 9:00 A.M. the guerrillas' lookouts brought word that Union troops were approaching. Quickly the raiders streamed out of town. They left behind only one of their own men dead; he was killed, not by any of the stunned citizens of Lawrence, but by an Indian whom he had been rash enough to cross. About one hundred and fifty men of Lawrence were dead. Even in the midst of such violence the moral code of the frontier was followed in one respect: not a single woman was molested.

A number of small bands of Kansans and some of the Kansas troops set out in pursuit of the guerrillas, capturing perhaps as many as a hundred of the stragglers and killing them on the spot. No prisoners were taken. But most of Quantrill's raiders were back in Missouri by nightfall.

General Order Number Eleven

Among the Kansans chasing Quantrill was the irate James H. Lane. While both federal troops and Kansans were still trying to locate the fleeing guerrillas, Lane had a stormy meeting with General Ewing. The general was in a bad position. As commander of the border district it was his job to prevent such forays, and the failure of his men to do so was not to his credit. Lane dictated an order that he demanded Ewing sign and informed the general that if he did not do so Lane would take political action to ruin him. Ewing reluctantly agreed to issue what became his General Order Number Eleven, requiring the removal of all people who did not live within a mile of a Union military post from three and one-half of the border counties of Missouri.

Lane immediately began a series of mass meetings in Kansas, whipping Kansans into a vengeful frenzy in preparation for an invasion of Missouri. General Schofield, the United States commander in Missouri, visited Lane and warned him that he would not permit Kansas troops to enter Missouri for revenge. Schofield was in a stronger position than Ewing and was possibly a stronger man; he did not give in to Lane's fury. Shortly afterward Lane headed a Congressional delegation that called upon President Lincoln and demanded Schofield's removal, but Lincoln stood behind the general.

To carry out General Order Number Eleven, the Missourians were given fifteen days to leave their homes. Despite Schofield's stand, Ewing permitted a Kansas organization led by Doc Jennison, the Fifteenth Kansas Cavalry, to be among those that enforced the order. Once again the operation became one of murder, looting, and destruction. A county that had had ten thousand people now had six hundred. The border area was completely devastated on the Missouri side and came to be known as "The Burnt District." Schofield stepped in and took the area away from Ewing's control, but by then the desolation was complete.

The extinction of three and one-half counties did have an effect on the guerrilla war. As Lane had foreseen, Missouri guerrillas no longer could use those counties as bases for raids into Kansas. The reverse was also true; there was no longer anything there to attract Kansas guerrillas into Missouri. Three other counties were later cleared of their inhabitants. Brutal and vengeful as was General Order Number Eleven, it greatly reduced irregular warfare along the border.

The Baxter Springs Massacre

That October Quantrill's men went south to spend the winter in Texas. They moved through Missouri and then crossed into Kansas at Baxter Springs in the extreme southeast corner of the state. Fort Baxter, a small Union post garrisoned by three companies, was located near Baxter Springs. Southward lay Indian territory. The first of the guerrillas to reach the fort attacked it and were driven off. In the meantime word came to Quantrill that a train of ten wagons was coming in from the north. He took part of his command and rode to meet it.

This was an important wagon train. In a buggy at the head of it was the Union general, James G. Blunt, who commanded the frontier district along the boundaries of Indian territory. He was escorted by one hundred cavalrymen and in one of the wagons there was a band. Mrs. Chester Thomas, the wife of an army contractor who was going to join her husband, rode with the general in his buggy.

Quantrill and some two hundred and fifty of his men formed a line facing the oncoming column. Many of them wore parts of Union uniforms. General Blunt concluded that this was an honor guard sent out by the fort to meet him, and he moved calmly toward them. When the two forces were sixty yards apart the guerrillas opened fire and then charged. The Union cavalry, taken completely by surprise, broke and ran, pursued in all directions by the guerrillas. General Blunt and Mrs. Thomas jumped from the buggy onto horses and escaped with a few of the soldiers. Quantrill's raiders took no prisoners. They killed nearly a hundred of Blunt's men. The unarmed musicians of the band, the teamsters, and the headquarters clerks were all killed, each one shot neatly in the head.

The guerrillas also captured an ambulance and all of the general's baggage, including his sword and flags. They had only three men killed

[74]

and four wounded. Destroying the wagons and putting one of their seriously wounded men in the ambulance, they headed out of Kansas into Indian territory.

The War Ends

That winter Quantrill's men quarreled and the group broke apart. Quantrill's former lieutenant, "Bloody Bill" Anderson, replaced him as the most important irregular leader in the West. They all returned to Missouri in 1864 to carry out guerrilla activities inside the state, but did little along the Kansas border. This was the training period for many of the outlaws who were to rob the banks and trains of western states after the war was over. Among the graduates of the guerrilla bands would be Coleman and James Younger and Frank and Jesse James.

"Bloody Bill" Anderson, who replaced Quantrill as the most important rebel leader in the West. (State Historical Society of Missouri)

[75]

The bloody decade in Kansas was a training ground for many future outlaws. Two of the most famous were Frank (left) and Jesse James. (State Historical Society of Missouri)

During 1864, while Sherman was marching to the sea in the East and Thomas was defeating Hood at Nashville, the war in the West at first centered in Arkansas. A number of Kansas troops were involved in normal military activities there. That fall the Confederacy was tottering. In a last attempt, General Sterling Price, the Confederate commander in the West, turned loose bands of prosouthern Indians to carry out raids along the borders of Indian territory while he took his army north again into Missouri. Governor Carney of Kansas called about twelve thousand Kansas militiamen to duty and imposed martial law along the borders. On October twenty-third Price was defeated by Union forces in Missouri at the Battle of Westport. He fell back through Kansas, fighting on October 25 the Battle of Mine Creek, the biggest battle fought on Kansas soil during the Civil War, and continued to retreat until he crossed the Arkansas River; there the Union pursuit ended. It was plain that the war was nearly over.

Guerrilla pickings were slim in Kansas and Missouri. Early in 1865 Qauntrill and thirty-three other men headed East, supposedly to assassinate President Lincoln. After John Wilkes Booth killed the President they no longer had any real aim. They moved about Kentucky for a time; there on May 10, Union soldiers found them asleep in a barn. Quantrill was shot trying to escape and was taken, seriously injured, to a Louisville hospital, where he died of his wounds on June 6.

Quiet at Last

After the Civil War the railroads started moving west through Kansas. The era of the Kansas cow towns followed. These were towns that sprang up along the growing rail lines to provide places of shipment for cattle that were driven north from Texas. Abilene, Newton, Wichita, Dodge City, and perhaps a dozen others flourished briefly. The history of most of them was the same. As long as the cow town was in unsettled territory it prospered. Then as settlers moved in around it and respectable merchants moved into it they quickly took steps to send the cattle and the trail drivers elsewhere. Large herds of cattle would ruin any farming area, and the gamblers, prostitutes, and saloon-keepers were no more the kind of people quiet businessmen and good townsfolk wanted around

Railroads moved westward through Kansas following the Civil War. These are rail yards at Wyandotte in 1867. (Kansas State Historical Society, Topeka)

than were the men who patronized them during the wild sprees that followed their arrival with cattle brought up the trails.

This was the era of Tom Smith, Wild Bill Hickok, Wyatt Earp, Bat Masterson, and the other frontier peace officers who tried with varying success to keep order in the cow towns. It was also the era of free-for-alls in the saloons and gunfights in the streets. Crowds of cowboys thronged the towns, celebrating the one visit they made to civilization —

or something like it —after many months of dull, hard work. All of them were out for a wild good time and many of them were drunk. Pistols and firearms were part of the working equipment of a trail driver and despite ordinances forbidding weapons in most towns, the ordinances, with a few exceptions, were not enforced.

Gun duels and plain murder were common, though not quite in the wholesale numbers suggested by television and Wild West fiction. A good deal of blood soaked into the Kansas soil in and around the cow towns. But gradually Kansas became what was envisioned when it first was made a territory, a settled area of prosperous farms. The farms moved slowly westward, quietly overwhelming the rowdy little cities, bringing people who set to work cleaning them up. In 1867 the first trainload of Texas cattle was shipped east from Abilene. By 1885 the last shipments went out of Dodge City, one hundred and fifty miles farther west.

Finally the area had settled down. The wars, battles, and gunfights were over and Kansas was quiet at last.

Bibliography

Bailey, L. D., *Border Ruffian Troubles in Kansas* (Lyndon, Kansas: privately printed, 1899).

Blackmar, Frank W., "A Chapter in the Life of Charles Robinson, the First Governor of Kansas," *Annual Report of the American Historical Association* (1894).

————, ed. *Kansas, A Cyclopedia of State History*, 2 vols. (Chicago: Standard Publishing Company, 1912).

Brownlee, Richard S., *Gray Ghosts of the Confederacy* (Baton Rouge: Louisiana State University Press, 1958).

Connelley, William E., "The Lane-Jenkins Claim Contest," *Collections of the Kansas State Historical Society*, XVI (1923–25).

————, *Quantrill and the Border Wars* (Cedar Rapids, Iowa: Torch Press, 1910).

————, *A Standard History of Kansas and Kansans*, vols. I and II, (Chicago: Lewis Publishing Company, 1918).

Craik, Elmer LeRoy, "Southern Interest in Territorial Kansas," *Kansas Historical Collections*, XV (1919–22).

Drago, Harry Sinclair, *Great American Cattle Trails* (New York: Dodd, Mead & Company, 1965).

Isely, W. H., "The Sharps Rifle Episode in Kansas History," *American Historical Review*, XII (October 1906–July 1907).

Klem, Mary J., "Missouri in the Kansas Struggle," *Proceedings of the Mississippi Valley Historical Association*, IX (1915–18).

Lynch, William U., "Popular Sovereignty and the Colonization of Kansas From 1854 to 1860," *Proceedings of the Mississippi Valley Historical Association*, IX (1915–18).

Malin, James C., *John Brown and the Legend of Fifty-Six* (Philadelphia: American Philosophical Society, 1942).

————, "The Proslavery Background of the Kansas Struggle," *Mississippi Valley Historical Review*, X (1923–24).

Moody, Ralph, *The Old Trails West* (New York: Thomas Y. Crowell Company, 1963).

Nevins, Allan, *Ordeal of the Union*, vol. II (New York: Charles Scribner's Sons, 1947).

Rhodes, James F., *History of the United States from the Compromise of 1850*, vol. II (New York: Harper and Brothers, 1893).

United States House of Representatives, *Report of the Special Committee Appointed to Investigate The Troubles in Kansas* (Washington, D. C.: C. Wendell, 1856).

Zornow, William Frank, *Kansas: A History of the Jayhawk State* (Norman, Okla.: University of Oklahoma Press, 1957).

Index

ABOUT THE AUTHOR

James P. Barry has written a number of books and articles on historical subjects, including two others in the Focus Books series. He has also done both the photography and writing for a picture book on the Great Lakes that is to be published soon.

A 1940 graduate of Ohio State University (cum laude, with distinction, Phi Beta Kappa), he entered the army in that same year as a lieutenant of of artillery. He served in the European theater of operations during World War II, then remained in the army for over twenty-five years, finally leaving it as a colonel. During that time he served in many places in the United States (including a tour in the Pentagon as senior editor for the Director of Army Intelligence) and abroad (including a tour as adviser to the Turkish army).

For several years he was a university administrator. He is now associated with an educational book publisher. Mr. Barry is a resident of Columbus, Ohio, and is married; his wife is a high-school librarian.